Enid Blyt

·BIBLE·STO

THE LC
AND FISHES

NEW TESTAMENT

GRAFTON BOOKS

A Division of the Collins Publishing Group

LONDON GLASGOW
TORONTO SYDNEY AUCKLAND

THE LOAVES AND FISHES

There was once a small boy who lived up in the hills that rose above the Lake of Galilee. He lived in a little white house with his mother and father and little sister. He was quite an ordinary little boy, who didn't dream that one day something wonderful was going to happen to him.

He helped his father on the hills, and he fetched water for his mother and sometimes looked after his little sister. Often he went fishing by himself, catching the fish in his hands, for he had no net.

One day he caught two little fish, and he was very proud of himself. He took them to his mother.

"Will you pickle these for me?" he asked her. She smiled at him.

"Yes, I will pickle them for you," she said. "And you shall eat them tomorrow. There will only be enough for you because they are so small."

So she pickled the two little fish and put them aside for the boy.

Now the next day the little boy was out on the hills with his little sister when he suddenly saw a great many people. They were streaming along the roads that led to the country round about the village of Bethsaida. The little boy had never seen so many people in the hills before.

He was astonished. Where had they all come from? And why were they there? Had something happened?

"I'm going to ask what's happened," the boy told his sister. "Stay here till I come back. What hundreds of people there are!"

He ran off to the crowds. "What's happened?" he asked. "Why have you all come here? There is nobody about here usually, except the villagers."

"We're looking for Jesus," said a woman. "He

set off in His boat across the lake with His disciples. So we've walked round the lake to find Him. He must be somewhere here. Have you seen Him?"

"Who is Jesus?" asked the little boy.

"Oh, haven't you heard of Him?" said another
boy. "He's a wonderful man. He can do miracles

and wonders! He can, really! He makes sick people well again and He can even make dead people alive. And there's another thing—He can tell the most marvellous stories. That's why *I've* come today. I love stories."

"So do I," said the boy from the hills. "I wish I could see this wonderful man and hear His stories. I think I'll go and ask my mother if I may."

He ran off home, and rushed into the house so fast that his mother looked up in surprise.

"Mother! Have you heard of a man called Jesus?" panted the boy. "He's somewhere in the hills nearby today. You should see the crowds that have come to hear Him! Mother, may I go and hear Him too? He tells stories and does miracles. I do so want to see Him."

"Very well," said his mother, smiling at the excited little boy. "Just wait a minute, though, and let me pack you up some food to take with you.

Look, here are five little loaves you can have—and wouldn't you like to take the two little fish you caught yesterday, that I have pickled for you?"

The boy could hardly wait for his mother to put his food into a small basket. He took it from her, said good-bye and ran off quickly.

The crowds were even bigger when he got up to them. "Is Jesus here?" he asked, anxiously. "I haven't missed Him, have I?"

"He's over on that grassy hillside," said a man. "His disciples are with Him."

Yes, Jesus was there. He had really come to these hills for a rest, because He was tired. But when He saw the crowds streaming along, He was sorry for them.

"They are like sheep without a shepherd," He said to His disciples, and He went to meet the people.

The little boy suddenly saw Him. He knew without a doubt that it was Jesus. He had never seen such clear, steady eyes before, such a wonderful face, or heard such a voice. So that was

Jesus, the man of wonders and miracles! The little boy took a deep breath, and gazed at Him in awe and wonder.

If only he could do something for this man! He was a hero to the little boy. If only Jesus would look at him and smile at him! But Jesus had so many people to see to, so much to do, that He didn't even look in the small boy's direction.

The disciples went here and there among the crowds, looking for sick, lame or blind people to bring to Jesus. The little boy saw them taken to Him, saw Him put His hands on them, and talk to them.

And behold they were well again, they could see, they could walk and run! They broke into shouts and songs of joy, and went down the hill, praising God and telling everyone what had happened to them.

Then Jesus sat down and began to preach.

The little boy listened. Jesus told some of His stories, and the lad strained his ears so that he should not miss a word.

"What wonderful stories!" he thought. "I can understand them all! I shall remember each one, and tell them to my mother and my little sister.

12

They will love them."

Jesus left His seat on the grassy hillside and went among the crowd, talking and healing once more. The boy followed Him at a distance, never losing sight of Him. What a wonderful day this was—so many people, so much to see—and this marvellous man in the middle of it all!

The boy had forgotten all about the food in the little basket his mother had given him. Usually he was very hungry and ate everything far too soon when he came out for the day. But today he had forgotten even to eat.

The day went by and the sun began to sink. Hundreds of people were still there in the hills, excited and happy. But they were beginning to get tired now, and most of them were very hungry, for they had not brought any food with them. They had walked a very long way, and now that they were hungry they wondered if there was

anywhere to buy food. But there were no shops in the hills.

The disciples went to Jesus. "Master," they said, "shall we send these people away and tell them to go into the villages and buy bread?"

"We must feed them," said Jesus.

"But Master—it would cost more than two hundred shillings to buy food for so many," said Philip, who was in charge of the money that the disciples had. "Do you wish us to go and buy food for the crowds?"

"Has no one here any food?" said Jesus. "Go and see." So the disciples went round the hillside, asking the same question over and over again.

"Has anyone food here? Who has brought food? Has anyone food here?"

But the people shook their heads. Either they had eaten what little they had brought, or they had forgotten to bring any in their excitement.

"Has anyone food here?" came the voices of the disciples, and the little boy heard the question too. He suddenly remembered the basket of food he had brought—the five little loaves and the two small fishes. He unwrapped them from the cloth in the basket and looked at them.

"I would so much like to give them to Jesus,"

thought the small boy. "I do so want to do something for Him, even if it's only a small thing. But would I dare to give these loaves and fishes to the disciples?"

He suddenly made up his mind. Yes, he would at least offer his food. So he pushed his way through the crowd and went up to one of the disciples.

"I have a little bread," he said. "And look, there are two small fishes as well. You can have them."

The disciple took the basket, and led the boy up to Jesus.

"Master," he said, "there is a lad here with five loaves and two fishes."

The boy was delighted to be so near the wonderful man he had been watching all the day. He looked up at Him shyly, his eyes wide with pleasure. Jesus smiled at him and took the basket from the disciple.

"Tell the people to sit down in companies of fifty so that we may feed them easily," He said to His disciples. The people obeyed, sitting down in big groups. The little boy watched in wonder. What was Jesus going to do?

Jesus took the five loaves from the basket and broke them. He looked up to heaven and blessed the bread He had broken. He gave it to His disciples. Then He divided the little fish and gave those to them as well.

The disciples came up one by one to get the food, and to the little boy's wonder and amazement, Jesus always had plenty for them.

He went on breaking up the bread and the fishes, giving out more and more, and the disciples came up time and again for another share to give to the hungry people.

"There is no end to my bread and fishes!" thought the little boy. "How can so little become

so much? This is a miracle I am watching. Jesus is doing a miracle with my five little loaves and two little fishes!"

There were five thousand people sitting on the hills and they were all fed. The disciples sat down to eat at last, and Jesus sat too, with the small boy

beside Him eating his own share, marvelling at every mouthful he took.

"Master," said the boy, shyly. "I caught these fish. And my mother baked the bread."

"I am glad you brought them and gave them to me," said Jesus, smiling at the small boy.

When everyone had eaten what they wanted, Jesus called His disciples and told them to go round and pick up all the scraps.

Nothing must be left to litter the lovely hillside and spoil it. The little boy went with the disciples, filling his own small basket with the scraps of bread and fish thrown down on the grass.

He looked at the baskets that were filled and counted them. "Twelve!" he said. "Twelve baskets full of scraps. And yet I only brought my own small basketful. Truly this is a very wonderful miracle. What will my mother say?"

It was time for everyone to go home. The sun

had set and soon it would be very dark. Jesus was in need of rest, and He wanted to pray to His Heavenly Father. He went silently into the hills alone.

The boy watched Him go. He had seen Jesus. He had listened to His stories. He had helped Him by giving Him his food. Jesus had smiled at him and spoken to him. He was the happiest boy in the world!

Now he must tell his mother all about it. She would hardly believe him! He ran up the hilly paths, panting. He was tired but very happy.

He came to his house at last. His mother was anxiously looking out for him. He flung himself on her.

"Mother, I saw Him! I saw Jesus! And do you know what happened to the five little loaves you baked, and the two fishes you pickled for me? Jesus took them and broke them and blessed

them—and Mother, there was enough to feed five thousand people! I saw a miracle done with my own bread and fishes!"

He told the wonderful story over and over again. "I shall never forget this day," he said. "It's been the greatest day of my life!"

·THE·END·